Famous Caves of the World ™

Mammoth Cave
The World's Longest Cave System

Brad Burnham

The Rosen Publishing Group's
PowerKids Press ™
New York

For Monica, Andrew, Mary, and Scott

Published in 2003 by Rosen Publishing Group, Inc.
29 East 21st Street, New York, NY 10010

Copyright © 2003 by The Rosen Publishing Group, Inc.

First Edition

Editor: Nancy MacDonell Smith
Book design: Michael J. Caroleo and Michael de Guzman

Photo Credits: Cover, title page, pp. 4, 8, 11, 15, 19, 20 © National Park Service; p. 7 © David Muench/CORBIS; pp. 12, 16 © Bettmann/CORBIS.

Burnham, Brad.
Mammoth Cave : the world's longest cave system / Brad Burnham.— 1st ed.
    p. cm. — (Famous caves of the world)
Includes bibliographical references and index.
Summary: Details the formation of the Mammoth Cave system of Kentucky and describes the natural wonders.
ISBN 0-8239-6258-X (library binding)
1. Mammoth Cave National Park (Ky.)—Juvenile literature. 2. Mammoth Cave (Ky.)—Juvenile literature. 3. Natural history—Kentucky—Mammoth Cave National Park—Juvenile literature. [1. Mammoth Cave National Park (Ky.) 2. Mammoth Cave (Ky.) 3. Caves. 4. National parks and reserves.] I. Title. II. Series.
    F457.M2 B97 2003
        551.44'7'09769754—dc21

                                                                            2001007773

Manufactured in the United States of America

Contents

KENTUCKY

Mammoth Cave

Under Kentucky Soil

In the south-central part of Kentucky, there is a series of caves that stretches for more than 350 miles (563 km) under ground. These connected caves make up the longest cave system in the world. Not all of this cave system has been explored. There may be 600 miles (966 km) of undiscovered caves! The government of the United States made this cave system into a national park in 1941. Mammoth Cave National Park includes the caves and 52,000 acres (21,044 ha) of land above ground. Many people visit the park each year to tour the caves. There are also activities above ground for visitors to enjoy. People can camp, hike in the park's woods, and canoe down the nearby rivers.

A series of walkways has been built in Mammoth Cave so that visitors can walk through the caves without harming the floors or walls.

Shaped by Water

The caves in Mammoth Cave National Park are made of **limestone**. They were formed by water that seeped into the ground and ate away at the limestone. This took place through millions of years.

Rainwater seeped into the ground and picked up **carbon dioxide** from the soil. When water is mixed with carbon dioxide, it becomes **carbonic acid**. Carbonic acid is a weak acid. It's similar to the acid found in soda. The carbonic acid entered cracks in the limestone and ate away at the rock. The acid made the cracks bigger and bigger until they became caves. Some of these water-filled cracks became underground rivers. One underground river that still flows today is called Echo River.

Over millions of years, the limestone in Mammoth Cave was shaped into amazing formations by water.

Long Avenues and Deep Pits

Water shaped the caves of Mammoth Cave National Park into long tunnels, known as avenues, and deep holes, called pits. One long tunnel is named Kentucky Avenue. It stretches for hundreds of feet (tens of meters) from one of the entrances to deep in the ground. Deep inside Mammoth Cave, Kentucky Avenue connects with Boone Avenue. Audubon Avenue and Cleveland Avenue are two other avenues in the cave system.

Water created holes by dripping on the same spot of the limestone for millions of years. The water made holes straight down into the rock. One of the deep holes near the Historic Entrance is known as the Bottomless Pit. It is 105 feet (32 m) deep. The Mammoth Dome is another deep pit. It is 192 feet (59 m) deep.

This park ranger is standing in Cleveland Avenue.

Beautiful Underground Shapes

Speleothems are shapes that form inside caves when water seeps through cracks in the walls and the ceilings. Water that seeps through the limestone walls and ceilings picks up **minerals** in the rock. The water carries these minerals into the cave and then leaves them on the ceilings and the walls. Through many years, the minerals build up and form large, beautiful shapes.

Stalactites are speleothems that hang down from the ceiling. Speleothems that rise up from the floor are called **stalagmites**, and **flowstones** are speleothems that cover objects on the walls and the floors. One large flowstone in Mammoth Cave is called Frozen Niagara. It's as tall as a large office building.

The Frozen Niagara flowstone resembles a waterfall that has frozen solid on a cold, winter day.

Miners of the Past

Some of the earliest human **explorers** of Mammoth Cave lived almost 4,000 years ago. Scientists have found **artifacts** that these people left behind. Artifacts have been found at least 10 miles (16 km) into the cave system.

These early explorers went into the cave to mine, or collect, minerals. We do not know why they collected minerals. They might have traded them with other people for goods.

People stopped mining in Mammoth Cave around 200 B.C., but, in the early 1800s, they started again. Deposits of **calcium nitrate** were mined and used as an ingredient in **gunpowder**. Today mining is not allowed anywhere in Mammoth Cave because the cave is a national park.

In 1876, when these drawings were made, Mammoth Cave was a tourist attraction, as well as a working mine.

Cave Life

Mammoth Cave is home to more than 130 different kinds of animals and insects. Some of the animals and insects have had to **adapt** to life in Mammoth Cave. It is too dark in the cave to see, so some kinds of animals have adapted by no longer having eyes. This adaptation is fine for living in caves, but is not very good for living outside of them. As a result, these animals never leave Mammoth Cave. They're called **troglodytes**, which means cave dwellers. A type of troglodyte is the eyeless fish.

Bats, crickets, and grasshoppers are not troglodytes because they sometimes leave the caves in which they live. They leave at night to find food on the ground or in the air. These animals are called **trogloxenes**, which means cave visitors.

Rangers give tours during which visitors can try to spot animals that live in Mammoth Cave, such as eyeless crayfish.

Early Tour Guides

In the early nineteenth century, visitors to Mammoth Cave were shown around the cave system by Stephen Bishop, Nick Bransford, and Mat Bransford. These men were slaves. They worked in the cave system and were knowledgeable about its many underground twists and turns. They had explored many parts of the cave system and knew it better than anyone else did.

Bishop and the Bransfords spent many years giving tours. They began a family practice of being tour guides for Mammoth Cave. When the three men retired, Mat's children became cave guides. Later Mat's grandchildren became tour guides, too. For more than 100 years, members of the Bransford family showed people around Mammoth Cave.

Bishop and the Bransfords took visitors through Mammoth Cave on small boats, which they rowed through the underground rivers.

Protecting the Cave

There are very few places on Earth like Mammoth Cave. In 1990, Mammoth Cave National Park was made into a biosphere reserve. This means it is protected from pollution and other human activities that may harm it.

Mammoth Cave National Park is not completely safe from pollution, though. Some pollution enters the park through the underground rivers. These rivers start outside of the park and can carry human waste and other pollution into the caves. People who live in communities near the park have been working with the National Park Service to lower the amount of pollution that enters the park. One way communities are doing this is by being more careful of how they get rid of their waste.

By protecting Mammoth Cave National Park from pollution, visitors and community members can save the park for everyone to enjoy.

Visitors to the Cave

Scientists who study the rocks, minerals, and animals found in caves are called speleologists. Scientists and students from Western Kentucky University are some of the speleologists who visit Mammoth Cave. They learn new things about the caves and share this information with other people. Other people visit the cave for fun. Rangers in Mammoth Cave National Park provide many different kinds of programs for people visiting the caves. One program is called Wild Caves. The people who join this program put on caving gear and explore some of the caves that are closed to most people. They crawl through tunnels and climb up and down ledges. These cavers have to wear helmets, kneepads, and coveralls.

It's hard to believe, but the tunnels that rangers lead visitors through were once tiny cracks in the ground!

Out in the Sunlight

The hiking trails and campsites at Mammoth Cave National Park allow visitors to get a feel for what is above ground, too. There are 73 miles (117 km) of trails for visitors to explore. Hikers in the woods can see sugar maple, white oak, and beech trees. They also might see traces of some of the animals that live there, such as white-tailed deer, raccoons, and chipmunks.

Mammoth Cave has miles (km) of enjoyment and beauty above and below ground. From frozen waterfalls and eyeless fish to hiking trails and chipmunks, there is something for everyone. It is a treasure that people from all over the world can enjoy.

Glossary

adapt (uh-DAPT) To change to fit new conditions.

artifacts (AR-tih-fakts) Objects created by humans.

calcium nitrate (KAL-see-um NY-trayt) A mineral found in the earth. It is an ingredient in gunpowder.

carbon dioxide (KAR-bin dy-OK-syd) A gas that the body makes to get rid of waste from energy that was used.

carbonic acid (kar-BON-ik A-sid) A kind of weak acid that forms when water mixes with carbon dioxide.

explorers (ik-SPLOR-urz) People who travel over undiscovered places.

flowstones (FLOH-stohnz) Layered deposits of calcium from thin flows of water.

gunpowder (GUN-pow-dur) A black powder that explodes in a gun and moves the bullet.

limestone (LYM-stohn) A kind of rock made mostly of calcium carbonate. It can be formed from the skeletons of small ocean organisms and coral.

minerals (MIN-ruhlz) Elements of which rocks are made.

speleothems (SPEE-lee-oh-thimz) Mineral formations inside of caves.

stalactites (stuh-LAK-tyts) A mineral formation, shaped like an icicle, that hangs from the roof of a cave.

stalagmites (stuh-LAG-myts) A mineral formation shaped like an icicle, that sticks up from the floor of a cave.

troglodytes (TRAH-gluh-dyts) An animal that has to live its whole life in a cave.

trogloxenes (TROG-le-zeenz) An animal that visits a cave or lives in it for part of its life.

Index

Web Sites

Due to the changing nature of Internet links, PowerKids Press has developed an online list of Web sites related to the subject of this book. This site is updated regularly. Please use this link to access the list:

www.powerkidslinks.com/fcow/mamm/